Woodland Animals

Raccoons

by William John Ripple

Consulting Editor: Gail Saunders-Smith, Ph.D.
Consultant: Daniel K. Rosenberg
Assistant Professor of Wildlife Ecology
Department of Forestry, Range, and Wildlife Sciences
Utah State University

Mankato, Minnesota

Pebble Books are published by Capstone Press,
151 Good Counsel Drive, P.O. Box 669, Mankato, Minnesota 56002.
www.capstonepress.com

1 2 3 4 5 6 11 10 09 08 07 06

Library of Congress Cataloging-in-Publication Data
Ripple, William John.
    Raccoons / by William John Ripple.
    p. cm.—(Pebble books. Woodland animals)
    Summary: "Simple text and photographs introduce the habitat, appearance, and
behavior of raccoons"—Provided by publisher.
    Includes bibliographical references and index.
    ISBN-13: 978-0-7368-4250-1 (hardcover)
    ISBN-10: 0-7368-4250-0 (hardcover)
    1. Raccoons—Juvenile literature. I. Title. II. Series.
QL737.C26R56 2006
599.76'32—dc22   2005018308

Note to Parents and Teachers

The Woodland Animals set supports national science standards
related to life science. This book describes and illustrates raccoons.
The photographs support early readers in understanding the text.
The repetition of words and phrases helps early readers learn new
words. This book also introduces early readers to subject-specific
vocabulary words, which are defined in the Glossary. Early readers
may need assistance to read some words and to use the Table of
Contents, Glossary, Read More, Internet Sites, and Index sections of
the book.

Table of Contents

What Are Raccoons?

Raccoons are mammals with thick fur.
Their faces look like black and white masks.

Raccoons are
gray and brown.

areas where raccoons live

Where Raccoons Live

Raccoons live in
North America,
Central America,
and South America.

Raccoons live in forests
and meadows.
Raccoons also live
near rivers and lakes.

Body Parts

Raccoons have
long, bushy tails
with black stripes.

14

Raccoons have
long fingers
that help them
catch and hold food.

What Raccoons Do

Raccoons climb trees
to find food.
They eat small animals,
eggs, seeds, and insects.

Raccoons sometimes dip their food in water before they eat it.

Raccoons hunt at night.
They sleep
during the day.

Glossary

forest—land covered mostly by trees; forests are also called woodlands.

hunt—to find and kill animals for food

insect—a small animal with six legs, three body sections, and two antennas

mammal—a warm-blooded animal with hair or fur; female mammals feed milk to their young.

meadow—a large open field of grass and other small plants

Read More

Jacobs, Lee. *Raccoon.* Wild America. San Diego: Blackbirch Press, 2003.

Nelson, Kristin L. *Clever Raccoons.* Pull Ahead Books. Minneapolis: Lerner, 2001.

Whitehouse, Patricia. *Raccoons.* What's Awake. Chicago: Heinemann Library, 2003.

Internet Sites

FactHound offers a safe, fun way to find Internet sites related to this book. All of the sites on FactHound have been researched by our staff.

Here's how:

1. Visit *www.facthound.com*
2. Type in this special code **0736842500** for age-appropriate sites. Or enter a search word related to this book for a more general search.
3. Click on the **Fetch It** button.

FactHound will fetch the best sites for you! 23

Index

Word Count: 95
Grade Level: 1
Early-Intervention Level: 10

Editorial Credits

Mari C. Schuh, editor; Patrick D. Dentinger, designer; Wanda Winch,
photo researcher; Scott Thoms, photo editor

Photo Credits

Aurora/Peter Essick, 20
Bruce Coleman Inc./Joe McDonald, 4; John Shaw, 6
Digital Vision/Peter Haigh, 8
Erwin and Peggy Bauer, 10, 12
Lynn M. Stone, 18
Photodisc/Geostock, 1
Tom and Pat Leeson, 14
U.S. Fish and Wildlife Service, 16
Visuals Unlimited/Steve Maslowski, cover

The author dedicates this book to his nephew Kail Vaith and niece Lindzie Vaith
of Lesterville, South Dakota.